A Rookery of
Penguins
and Other Bird Groups

Jilly Hunt

www.raintreepublishers.co.uk
Visit our website to find out more information about Raintree books.

To order:
☎ Phone 0845 6044371
🖹 Fax +44 (0) 1865 312263
🖳 Email myorders@raintreepublishers.co.uk

Customers from outside the UK please telephone +44 1865 312262

Raintree is an imprint of Capstone Global Library Limited, a company incorporated in England and Wales having its registered office at 7 Pilgrim Street, London, EC4V 6LB – Registered company number: 6695582

Text © Capstone Global Library Limited 2013
First published in hardback in 2013
Paperback edition first published in 2014
The moral rights of the proprietor have been asserted.

Edited by Nancy Dickmann, Adam Miller, and Laura Knowles
Designed by Richard Parker
Original illustrations © Capstone Global Library Ltd 2013
Illustrations by Jeff Edwards
Picture research by Ruth Blair
Originated by Capstone Global Library Ltd
Printed and bound in China by CTPS

ISBN 978 1 406 23950 8 (hardback)
16 15 14 13 12
10 9 8 7 6 5 4 3 2 1

ISBN 978 1 406 23957 7 (paperback)
17 16 15 14 13
10 9 8 7 6 5 4 3 2 1

British Library Cataloguing in Publication Data
Hunt, Jilly.
A rookery of penguins and other bird groups. -- (Animals in groups)
598.1'56-dc22
A full catalogue record for this book is available from the British Library.

Acknowledgements
We would like to thank the following for permission to reproduce photographs: Corbis p. 29 (© Tim Davis); Dreamstime.com pp. 4 (© Goinyk Volodymyr), 13 (© Gentoomultimedia), 26 (© Bernard Breton), 34 (© Adeliepenguin); iStockphoto pp. 9 (© saluha), 15 (© thp73), 17 (© MOF), 19 (© Marshall Bruce), 24 (© Mogens Trolle), 25, 27 (© Keith Szafranski), 37 (© doubleus), 40 (© Focus_on_Nature); Naturepl pp. 12, 21 (© Fred Olivier), 22 (© Charlie Summers), 23 (© Andy Rouse), 30 (© Doug Allen); Photolibrary pp. 18 (Michel Gunther/BIOS), 35 (Animals Animals); Shutterstock pp. 5 (© Karel Gallas), 7 (© Bruno Medley), 11 (© Moritz Buchty), 16, 41 (© Volodymyr Goinyk), 33 (© Sean Nel), 38 (© David Steele), 39 (© EcoPrint).

Cover photograph of king penguins at Volunteer Point, Falkland Islands reproduced with permission of Shutterstock (© kwest).

Every effort has been made to contact copyright holders of any material reproduced in this book. Any omissions will be rectified in subsequent printings if notice is given to the publisher.

Disclaimer

Contents

DID YOU KNOW?

Discover amazing facts about penguins.

Some words are shown in bold, **like this**. You can find out what they mean by looking in the glossary.

HUMAN INTERACTION

Find out what happens when humans and penguins come into contact with each other.

HABITAT IN DANGER

Learn how penguins' habitats are under threat, and what is being done to protect them.

Welcome to the rookery!

A rookery is the name for a group of penguins. Sometimes, the group is also called a colony. Penguins are a type of seabird. There are nearly 9,800 **species** (types) of bird, but only about 300 of these species are seabirds.

This chinstrap penguin lives in a cold climate.

DID YOU KNOW?

The biggest penguin is the emperor penguin. It can grow up to 130 centimetres (51 inches) tall. The smallest penguin is the Little penguin, which only grows up to about 40 centimetres (16 inches) tall.

There are at least 17 different species of penguins. The various species of penguins live in different places and look slightly different from each other. Many species of penguin live in very cold places around Antarctica. Antarctica is the south **polar** region of the world, which is almost entirely covered by ice. Some species of penguin live in warmer or even hot places, such as the Galápagos Islands near South America.

The African penguin lives in warmer areas, such as South Africa.

HUMAN INTERACTION

Many people are familiar with penguins from seeing them in films and books, or at zoos or wildlife parks. However, most people will never see a wild penguin. This is because most penguins live in very remote places.

Are penguins like other birds?

All birds have some basic features in common, even though they might look completely different. A penguin doesn't look exactly like an owl or a parrot, but they are all birds.

Some of the characteristics that all birds share are that:
- they are warm-blooded
- they have an outer covering of feathers
- they have wings
- they lay eggs.

Birds are alone in having feathers – no other animals have them. Birds are endothermic, which means they are warm-blooded. This means that their body temperature stays the same even when the outside temperature changes. That is why penguins can live in places as cold as Antarctica. A penguin does have wings, called flippers, but it cannot fly. A penguin uses its flippers for swimming. If you see a penguin underwater, it looks like it is flying through the water.

DID YOU KNOW?

Scientists group plants and animals to help understand them better. This is called classification. Through classification and research, scientists can tell that penguins are from an old order, or group, of birds that date back to the time of the dinosaurs.

Feathers are so important to a penguin that they must be carefully looked after. Some penguins spend up to three hours a day **preening** their feathers to keep them healthy and waterproof.

Body parts

Penguins have **adapted** to suit their environment. This means they have developed features that help them survive where they live. For example, penguins have webbed feet, just like ducks. Their webbed feet help them to steer underwater. The claws on a penguin's webbed feet help it to grip on to slippery rocks or ice when it is getting out of the ocean. The claws are also useful when a penguin pushes itself along ice on its tummy. Claws are even used to dig **burrows** to nest in.

Penguins spend a lot of time in the water, so their feathers must be waterproof. They overlap very closely, a bit like the scales on a fish, to keep water out. Penguins also make oil in their bodies which they spread over their feathers to stop them letting in water.

Penguin wings are shorter than those of most birds, and act more like paddles. Their flippers help them dive more easily.

DID YOU KNOW?

The coloured markings on a penguin help **camouflage** it. A leopard seal out hunting for penguins will find it difficult to see the white tummy of a penguin if it's looking up against the light of the sky. Similarly, if the leopard seal is looking down into the darker depths of the ocean, it will be harder to see the penguin's black back.

Penguins have adapted to suit their **habitat**. Each body part helps this king penguin to survive.

beak for catching **prey**

shape of the beak depends on what the penguin eats

white and black feathers for camouflage

feathers trap a layer of air which helps keep penguins warm

tail to steer underwater

webbed feet for steering and braking underwater

claws for gripping

9

Where do penguins live?

Birds live all over the world. Some birds stay in one area, while others **migrate** around the world depending on the season. Birds may migrate to find food, to return to a **breeding** area, or to find better conditions. Birds often migrate along the same routes year after year.

Some types of penguins migrate. They return to the colony where they were hatched to **moult** and breed. Other penguins are called "resident species". This means they stay in the same area all year round.

Southern hemisphere

All penguins in the wild live in the southern **hemisphere**. Many penguins live in **sub-Antarctic** regions. There are some species which live in warmer areas such as South Africa and New Zealand. The Galápagos penguin lives near the **equator**, where it is very hot.

Remote regions

Penguins usually live in remote regions where there are no land **predators**. Penguins cannot fly, and they cannot run quickly, so it is safer for them if there are no land predators. However, penguins spend most of their lives at sea because this is where they catch their food.

HABITAT IN DANGER

The Galápagos penguins rely on cold ocean **currents** to bring their food supply. These currents are sometimes disrupted by a change in the weather patterns which can leave penguins facing big food shortages, and even death.

The Galápagos penguin is a year-round resident of the Galápagos Islands.

Adaptations for cold weather

Penguins have certain adaptations and behaviours that help them to stay warm or keep cool. For example, a penguin's feathers are very important in keeping it warm. Most birds have some gaps between feathers but the penguin doesn't. This helps to create a windproof outer shell and to stop cold water from seeping through. Penguins also have a special type of feather that traps a layer of air which helps keep them warm.

Animals that live in cold places have to make sure they don't lose heat. They are usually larger than other animals. The biggest penguins – emperor penguins – are those that live in the coldest areas. The smallest penguins – the Galápagos and the Little penguin – live in the warmest areas.

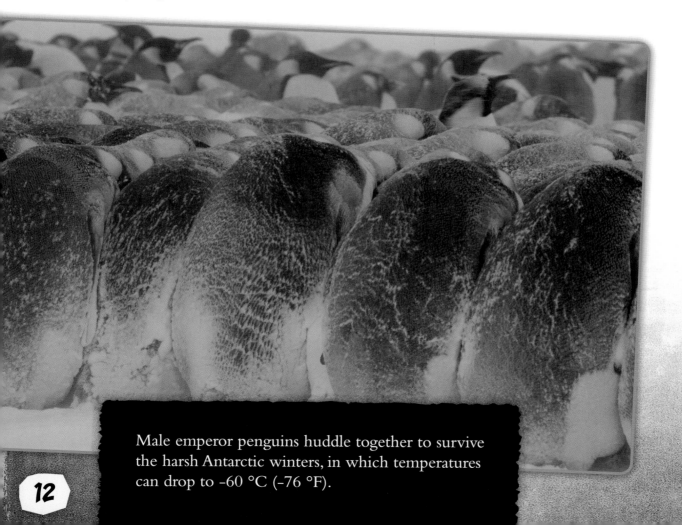

Male emperor penguins huddle together to survive the harsh Antarctic winters, in which temperatures can drop to –60 °C (–76 °F).

Behaviours

Penguins use their feet and flippers to help maintain their body temperature. African penguins lie at the surface of the ocean first thing in the morning with one flipper and one foot held up to the Sun. The heat from the Sun helps them to warm up.

Male emperor penguins huddle together to protect themselves against the cold. They form a "turtle" shape with the males on the outside gradually moving in to the centre, and the ones on the inside gradually moving outwards. They take turns standing on the outside, which is the coldest place.

Sometimes penguins get too hot and have to cool off under running water or by jumping in the ocean for a cooling swim.

DID YOU KNOW?

When it gets too hot, the Magellanic penguins along the coast of Patagonia pant to cool off.

13

Where do penguins lay their eggs?

Most penguins return to the colony where they hatched to breed and lay their eggs. This usually happens in late spring, when the weather is better. There is enough food for all the returning penguins at this time of year.

Nests

Most penguin colonies are on level or slightly sloping ground, but some types of penguin build their nests on rocky coastline. Some penguins nest on top of the ground in a shallow, open area that they have scraped. Others dig a burrow, or find a hole in a rock. King and emperor penguins don't have a nest. They keep their one egg on top of their feet to keep it warm and safe.

Penguins remember where they nested the year before and go back there. Some breeding sites are around 4,000 to 5,000 years old. The Adélie penguin actually returns to the same nest made of pebbles that it had the year before.

DID YOU KNOW?

Adélie penguins will steal pebbles from their neighbours whenever they can to make their nests better.

By nesting in colonies, penguins can tell each other where food is. It is also easier for a colony to defend its nests from flying predators, such as skuas and petrels.

Finding a mate

A male penguin builds a nest to attract a female. He then puts on a **display** to get himself noticed. When choosing a **mate**, a female penguin looks for one who is colourful – this means he is healthy. She also looks for large males, since they will probably be able to defend their nest. A male who is fat must know how to find food, which will be useful for feeding the chick.

Most penguins keep the same mate as the previous year. If they don't, it could be because one penguin has died, or they have not turned up to the breeding site at the same time.

This penguin is putting on a display to impress a partner. He puffs out his chest and flings back his head and flippers.

Sometimes penguins decide not to breed the next year because they do not get on with each other successfully. For example, some pairs cannot **incubate** their eggs properly. Penguins may also separate if one partner doesn't turn up at the nest, forcing the other to leave it to look for food to feed the chicks. If this happens, the breeding season is lost. The penguins won't mate again the following season.

Fighting

Penguins sometimes fight with each other at breeding time. A male will fight if he finds his old nest being used by another male, particularly if the other male has taken his partner, too. Males will fight by bumping chests, beating each other with their flippers, or wrestling with their sharp beaks. Females will also fight if they find another female has taken their mate.

Although penguins can hurt each other when fighting, serious injuries are rare.

Building a bond

When a penguin has found a mate they start to form a **bond**, or relationship, together. Both male and female penguins work together to look after their eggs and raise their chicks, so a strong bond between parents is important.

Penguins use displays and calls to build a bond with each other. Each species has its own calls and displays. One thing they have in common is that they all try not to be frightening. They do this by hiding their bills and by bowing. Penguins will also "sing" duets as part of their **courtship**.

Some penguins will also preen each other's feathers to get rid of fleas and ticks. Courting penguins will also fix up their nests. They use grass, seaweed, sticks, bones, pebbles, and feathers.

"Singing" together helps the male and female penguins form a strong bond.

HABITAT IN DANGER

Global warming will affect many penguin species. Scientists believe it will melt much of the sea-ice that penguins such as the emperor penguin breed on.

Mating

Once the bond has been made, the penguin pair will quickly mate. It is then back to preening and collecting more nesting material.

Most penguin species will only breed once a year. The Galápagos penguin may breed twice in one year. King penguins may breed twice in three years because they have a longer breeding cycle.

The orange patches on a male king penguin's neck are an important signal. They tell the female he is healthy.

How do penguins look after their eggs?

Birds don't give birth to live young like humans and other **mammals** do. Instead, they lay eggs. Like most seabirds, penguins lay only a few eggs at a time because the parents are not able to provide enough food for more than one or two chicks. King and emperor penguins lay only one egg.

Keeping the eggs warm

Keeping the eggs warm is called incubation. In all penguin species except the emperor, the males and females take it in turns to incubate the eggs. One parent can go off to feed while the other stays with the eggs. The eggs must be kept warm or the chicks inside will get cold and die.

Penguins incubate their eggs by keeping them close to their bodies. Penguin parents lose feathers from a small area on their lower bellies called a brooding patch. The parents keep their eggs close to this patch so as to warm them with their body heat. Penguin feathers do such a good job of keeping the heat in that if the parents didn't lose their feathers, the eggs wouldn't be warmed by the parent's body heat.

DID YOU KNOW?

The male emperor penguin holds the record for the longest continuous incubation. He incubates his egg for 64 days without ever leaving it. He looks after the egg through the freezing cold winter and won't eat for 15 weeks or more until the female returns.

The female emperor penguin lays one egg, and then it is carefully moved across to the male.

Hatching

Penguin chicks get no help from their parents when it is time to get out of their eggs. Penguin chicks, like other birds, have an egg tooth. This is a hard part on the tip of the beak, which the chick uses to chip its way through the thick shell. The chick can be heard cheeping before the shell has cracked. Although the parents don't help, they are very interested and will leave bits of food on the hatching shell.

DID YOU KNOW?

A king penguin chick hatches with no feathers at all. It will grow **down** feathers within a few weeks.

It takes one to three days for a penguin chick to hatch out of its shell. This is longer than most birds, probably because a penguin egg shell is so thick.

Penguin chicks

Most newly hatched penguin chicks are covered with very fine feathers called down. The colour of the down depends on the species of penguin. Some are silver-grey, while others are dark brown or black. They look very different from their parents.

A penguin parent can recognize its own chick's call from all the other chicks.

HUMAN INTERACTION

Tourists and scientists wanting to see and study penguins can actually cause them harm. The penguins get disturbed by people and may leave their nests. When the parents aren't there, a bird called a skua may take the opportunity to feed on the young chicks.

Looking after the young

When the egg is due to hatch, the parents take shorter turns at incubating the egg so they can keep their bellies full, ready to feed the new chick. Sometimes a full-bellied parent won't arrive for a few days. When a penguin chick hatches, a parent will try to feed it. The parent does this by **regurgitating** food. This means the parent brings up food that it has already swallowed and puts it in the chick's open mouth.

Most chicks can survive two to three days by feeding on the inner part of the egg they hatched from. The penguin chick and its parents will recognize each other through their calls. A penguin will only feed its own chick.

A penguin chick puts its head right up into the throat of its parent so food is not lost.

A male emperor penguin may have eaten nothing for months while incubating his egg. Yet he is still able to regurgitate a kind of **curd** which is rich in fat and protein for the little chick. A chick can survive for up to two weeks after hatching, just on its father's curd. Then they have to wait for the female to return with food. If she doesn't return it is likely that the chick will die because the father will leave to find food.

Penguin chicks will beg for food from any adults.

DID YOU KNOW?

If there are two eggs, the first one to hatch becomes the stronger chick because it gets fed first. The second, smaller, chick often dies. Sometimes its sibling attacks and kills it.

Growing up

Some penguin species grow more quickly than others. For example, a Galápagos penguin will become fully **fledged** after 65 days. A king penguin chick takes 10 to 13 months to fledge.

A penguin chick's eyelids are sealed shut for about three to four days after it hatches. Its parents will constantly guard it by covering it with their bodies. By the second week, the chick is bigger and the parent just crouches over it. By the third week, the chick sits next to its parent but will still try to hide under the adult if it gets scared. By the fourth week, the chick begins to explore around the nest.

It takes about two to three weeks for a chick's down feathers to be thick enough to keep them warm. In the meantime, they must shelter by their parents to keep warm.

When the chick has moulted it will leave the colony to find its own food at sea.

Finding enough food

When the chicks are old enough, both parents will leave them to search for food at sea. For some penguin species, the chicks stay by themselves in the nest. For other species, such as king and emperor penguins, chicks crowd together in groups called **crèches**, often in the middle of the colony for protection.

When the penguin chick is about two to five months old it stops being fed by its parents. The chicks watch the adults coming and going to sea. At this stage, the chicks moult and lose their down feathers to reveal their adult feathers.

Penguin chicks are safer from predators in a crèche.

27

What do penguins eat?

When a penguin chick has left the nest it must start to find its own food. It also must try to avoid becoming food for something else!

All penguins eat three main foods: fish, squid, and crustaceans (animals with hard shells) such as krill. Penguins that live around the Southern Ocean must dive deep down to look for fish. Those penguins that live in warmer areas often catch fish closer to the surface. Penguin mouths have spines inside which help them hold on to their slippery prey.

Group work

By working as a group, penguins are more likely to find food. Krill and fish are often scattered around in the sea. One penguin may struggle to find food by itself, but by sharing information with the colony there is a better chance of more birds getting food.

Penguins prefer to travel in groups because there is less risk from predators. Groups of penguins seem to watch for the safe arrival of other large groups of penguins before they go out hunting. This means that there is less likely to be a predator waiting under water to attack them.

HUMAN INTERACTION

In the warmer regions, penguins compete with humans over the fish supply. Humans fish for anchovies, sardines, and pilchards to eat and sell. These are the same fish penguins eat.

Penguins swim and feed in groups, but most make dives to catch their food alone.

Predators

Killer whales, leopard seals, fur seals, and sea lions will all hunt penguins. They swim near the penguin colonies in the hope of catching penguins when they go to sea.

A leopard seal will wait underwater to attack penguins jumping into the sea.

On land, some penguins are at risk from animals such as foxes and snakes. For example, in the Galápagos Islands, crabs and snakes eat penguin eggs. Other seabirds, such as sheathbills, are also a threat to penguins.

Living in a rookery can help protect penguins. A large group is better at spotting a skua flying overhead and then fighting it off. In addition, a large rookery of penguins whose chicks are all at the same age means that the predators have too much possible prey. There are only so many chicks a predator can kill, so more chicks overall will survive.

Food chains and webs

Penguins are an important part of the food chains and webs in their **ecosystems**. A food chain is a series of living things in which each animal feeds on the one before. A food web is made up of a group of food chains within one ecosystem.

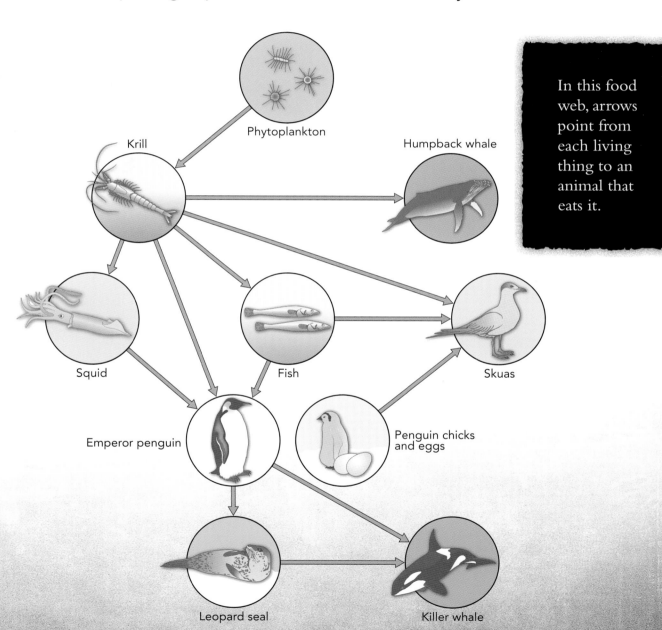

Phytoplankton

Krill

Humpback whale

Squid

Fish

Skuas

Emperor penguin

Penguin chicks and eggs

Leopard seal

Killer whale

In this food web, arrows point from each living thing to an animal that eats it.

Are penguins in danger?

Penguins are at risk in a number of ways. Their natural predators are a threat, but humans can also put penguins in danger.

Sometimes humans don't realize that their activities are causing penguins harm. For example, an aircraft flying over a penguin colony can scare them and cause panic. The penguins may stampede, resulting in injuries, broken eggs, and easier prey for predators. Tourists and scientists may also disturb penguins.

Some people may eat penguins or use them to catch other animals. Collecting penguin eggs is banned, but some people still do this. Penguins can also be disturbed by human activity such as road construction and building developments. On a small group of islands in the Indian Ocean called the Crozet Islands, a whole colony of king penguins was destroyed because of human building activity.

HUMAN INTERACTION

In places such as Australia and New Zealand, humans have created a new danger for penguins. They have introduced animals into the countryside which are not part of the natural world in these areas. Rats, ferrets, stoats, dogs, and cats are not penguins' natural predators, but all will eat penguin eggs.

You can help the survival of penguins by telling your friends and family all about them. The more people who know about penguins and the dangers they face, the more likely it is that humans will stop their harmful activities. You could also support a wildlife charity, such as the WWF. See page 46 for more details.

People also compete with penguins for food. Too much fishing can threaten penguin numbers as there is not enough food to go round.

Threats to habitats

Global warming is affecting many penguin habitats. Global warming is the rise in average air temperatures near the surface of Earth. The change in temperature affects the weather and ocean currents. Penguins rely on certain ocean currents to bring in their food supply. If these currents change, penguins can be left with food shortages and many may die.

Global warming also means that the polar **ice caps** are melting. As the ice melts, some penguin species, especially the emperor penguins, are losing important habitats. Less sea ice also affects the number of krill which feed just below the ice. This means less food for the penguins.

Some parts of the Antarctic would become ice-free with a global temperature increase of just 2 degrees Celsius (3.6 degrees Fahrenheit).

HUMAN INTERACTION

In 1936, scientists experimented to see whether penguins could live in the Arctic, as conditions seemed to be similar to the Antarctic. Nine king penguins were released into the wild, followed by several chinstrap and macaroni penguins two years later. However, the experiments were a disaster. None survived. One king penguin was clubbed to death by a local woman who thought it was a demon, one drowned when it got hooked on a fishing line, and another died when its feathers got covered in oil.

Pollution

Penguins are also at risk from **pollution**. Rubbish in the ocean can affect all seabirds and sea life. Penguins have accidentally eaten plastic or become tangled up in rubbish and died.

Oil spills greatly affect penguins and can kill them. The oil sticks to their feathers, which makes them less waterproof and not so good at keeping the birds warm. Penguins can die if they get too cold. Penguins may also be poisoned by the oil when they are preening their feathers.

Penguins die from being covered in oil leaked from ships and pipelines.

Do other birds live in groups?

Penguins are not the only birds that live in groups. Many species of birds live in colonies. These include seabirds in the Alcidae family, which look similar to penguins. This family of birds includes puffins, auks, auklets, guillemots, and murres.

Northern look-alikes

Although penguins live in the southern hemisphere, puffins, murres, and auklets live in the northern hemisphere. These birds have black and white colouring like penguins. The puffin also has brightly coloured markings which are similar to penguins. Like penguins, these birds fish for food under water using their wings to push them along. However, unlike penguins, they can fly, too.

Group behaviour

Birds in the Alcidae family breed in colonies and usually mate for life. Both male and female birds incubate the eggs and feed the young. Alcidae family birds have land predators such as rats, so they choose nesting sites that are hard to get to. For example, puffins nest in crevices on rocky islands. Murres nest on cliff ledges. Most of these birds lay their eggs on the ground or in a burrow, just like penguins.

HABITAT IN DANGER

The habitat of many seabirds, such as the puffin, is threatened by pollution, especially oil spills. Overfishing is also a big threat to these birds.

Puffins live in colonies in the northern hemisphere.

Weavers

Weavers are a group of birds that seem very different from penguins. However, the weavers are very social birds and live in groups. They have an interesting way of building their colonies.

Weavers are small birds that live on **savannahs**, grasslands, and other open habitats in Africa and southern Asia. Like most birds, weavers can fly. Weavers live in groups that can be so large that when they fly together they look like dark clouds of smoke.

This brightly coloured male Cape weaver lives in South Africa.

Unlike penguins, the male has more than one mate at a time. He builds a nest, attracts a female to it, and then starts another nest to attract another female.

After breeding, weavers will form flocks that contain birds from different species. They often fly long distances to find food. Weavers eat seeds and insects from the ground.

Social weavers work together in pairs to build very fancy nests with straw. These enormous nests are built in trees and may contain 100 chambers. Each pair has its own chamber. The nest has a roof which covers the whole colony. The roof may be up to 4.5 metres (15 feet) wide and 3 metres (10 feet) high. The social weaver's nest is the largest nest built by any bird.

The straw roof of the social weavers' colony keeps the nest cool in the day but warm at night.

HABITAT IN DANGER

There are seven weaver species that are considered **endangered**. Bannerman's weaver and Bates' weaver are both found in forests in Cameroon, Africa. Their habitats are threatened and so the birds are at risk.

Why do penguins live in rookeries?

Penguins are fascinating birds that achieve some amazing feats. Even though they cannot fly, they are skilled swimmers. Some species, such as the emperor, survive incredibly harsh conditions.

Living in a rookery helps penguins and other birds survive. The rookeries give penguins the advantage of safety in numbers. Living in a large group allows penguins to work together to raise chicks and fight off predators.

Penguin rookeries are also social groups. They provide a place where penguins can return each year to breed. The penguins can communicate with each other about where there are good sources of food. Other birds that live in groups do so for similar reasons.

It is best not to get this close to penguins – they are safest when left alone.

Different types of nest

Bird colonies can be very different. Penguins make simple nests in the ground from pebbles, or they may dig burrows. Other birds that live in colonies may make more complicated nests. Social weaver birds make huge nests out of straw. Around 600 birds live there.

Penguins are wonderful birds that live in some of the world's harshest environments.

HUMAN INTERACTION

Some penguins are in danger of **extinction**, but all penguins (and other wildlife) are in danger from pollution and global warming. You can help fight global warming by doing some simple things such as not leaving lights on when you are not in a room, and by recycling your rubbish.

41

Fact file

PENGUINS

Number of species of penguins: about 17

Species that migrate: Rockhopper, Fiordland, Snares, erect-crested penguin, macaroni, royal, magellanic, Adélie, emperor, king

Species that are resident: Humboldt, Galápagos, African or Jackass, gentoo, yellow-eyed, little or fairy penguin

Breeding season: Depends on species

Number of eggs laid: 1–2 eggs

Main food eaten: fish, squid, and krill

Predators include: Killer whales, leopard seals, fur seals, sea lions, foxes, snakes, crabs, skuas, caracaras, sheathbills, giant petrels

Depth they can dive to: Most can dive to at least 100 metres (328 feet). Emperor penguins can dive to over 600 metres (nearly 2000 feet).

Length of time they can hold their breath: most can hold their breath for five to six minutes. Emperor penguins can hold their breath for up to 22 minutes!

Endangered species: Yellow-eyed penguin, Northern Rockhopper penguin, erect-crested penguin, African penguin, and Galápagos penguin

Vulnerable species: Southern Rockhopper penguin, Macaroni penguin, Fiordland penguin, Snares penguin, Royal penguin, Humboldt penguin

PUFFINS

Part of the Alcidae family with auks, guillemots, and murres
Nest in large colonies on cliffs
Breeding season: February to early April
Number of eggs laid: usually one egg
Main food: fish, sea eels, and other sea animals
Predators include: gulls and skuas, rats and other ground mammals
Conservation: not considered to be at risk

WEAVERS

Part of the Ploceidae family
Build large nests in trees
Breeding season: any time of the year, linked to rainfall
Main food: seeds and insects
Endangered species: Mauritius Fody, Gola Malimbe, Ibadan Malimbe, Golden-naped weaver, Bates' weaver, Clarke's weaver, Usambara weaver, Loango weaver
Vulnerable species: Rodrigues Fody, Bannerman's weaver, Kilombero weaver, Yellow-legged weaver, Yellow weaver

This map shows you where penguins live around the world.

where penguins live

Glossary

adapted way a type of plant or animal has changed gradually to help it survive in its environment

bond close relationship

breeding having young

burrow hole or tunnel dug by an animal for shelter

camouflage colours and patterns that help an animal's body blend in with its background

courtship behaviour that leads to mating and having young

crèche group of baby penguin chicks

curd fatty substance made by a father penguin to feed its newly hatched chick

current movement of sea water in a particular direction

display show of actions to send a message to other animals

down soft, fine feathers that help keep birds warm

ecosystem living and non-living things in a particular area

endangered at risk of dying out

equator imaginary line around the middle of Earth

extinction dying out

fledge when a bird becomes old enough to look after itself

global warming gradual increase in the temperature of Earth's atmosphere

habitat natural home or surroundings of a living thing

hemisphere half of Earth. The northern hemisphere is north of the equator and the southern hemisphere is south of the equator.

ice cap covering of ice over a large area

incubate when a bird sits on its eggs to keep them warm

mammal hairy animal that feeds its young with milk from the mother's body

mate partner that an animal has babies with

migrate when an animal moves to a different area as the seasons change

moult lose feathers

polar relating to the North or South Pole

pollution harmful or poisonous things in the environment

predator animal that hunts and eats other animals

preening cleaning and tidying feathers

prey animal that is hunted and eaten by another animal

regurgitate bring food back up from the stomach

savannah grassy plain

species particular type of living thing

sub-Antarctic area immediately north of the Antarctic circle

Find out more

Books

100 Facts on Birds, Jinny Johnson and Belinda Gallagher (Miles Kelly Publishing, 2007)

100 Facts on Penguins, Camilla de la Bedoyere (Miles Kelly Publishing, 2009)

Polar Regions (Habitat Survival), Melanie Waldron (Raintree, 2013)

Who Counts the Penguins?: Working in Antarctica (Wild Work), Mary Meinking (Raintree, 2011)

Websites

www.bbc.co.uk/nature/life/Emperor_Penguin
Discover more about emperor penguins and watch videos of them in their natural habitat.

www.wwf.org.uk
Find out more about wildlife and what is being done to help protect species at risk.

www.arkive.org/birds
Discover more about penguins and other birds and see photos and videos on this website.

DVDs

Frozen Planet, David Attenborough (BBC, 2011)

Life in the Freezer, David Attenborough (BBC, 2002)

March of the Penguins, Luc Jacquet (Warner, 2005)

Places to visit

Find out if your nearest wildlife park or zoo has penguins you can visit. Or look in your garden, local park, or school grounds to see if you can spot birds that live closer to home. Here are two wildlife parks that specialize in penguins and other birds:

Birdworld
Holt Pound, Farnham,
Surrey, GU10 4LD
www.birdworld.co.uk

Living Coasts
Torquay Harbourside
Beacon Quay, Torquay
Devon, TQ1 2BG
www.livingcoasts.org.uk

More topics to research

Think about what you enjoyed finding out about most in this book. The emperor penguin goes through a remarkable feat of endurance to survive the Antarctic winter. Perhaps you could discover more about what it goes through by watching the *March of the Penguins* DVD? Or perhaps you enjoyed learning about the ways penguins keep warm or cool off. See if you can find out more information in books at your local library or on the internet.

Index